Performers in Uniform

NAVAL SPECIAL WARFARE TEAMS

By Peter B. Mohn

Photographs courtesy of the U.S. Navy

Consultant:
   Commander Ron Yeaw
   Naval Special Warfare, Group II

 CHILDRENS PRESS, CHICAGO

Library of Congress Cataloging in Publication Data

Mohn, Peter B
  Naval special warfare teams.

  (Performers in uniform)
  SUMMARY: Describes the specialized training and
work of the divers, parachutists, and frogmen of the
Navy's special warfare teams.
  1.United States. Navy. Underwater Demolition
Teams—Juvenile literature. 2.United States.
Navy. Sea Air Land Team—Juvenile literature.
3.United States. Navy. Basic Underwater Demolition School—Juvenile literature. [1.United
States. Navy. Underwater Demolition Teams.
2.United States. Navy. Sea Air Land Team.
3.United States. Navy. Basic Underwater Demolition School] I. Title.
VG87.M63   359.9'84'0973   80-26004
ISBN 0-516-01955-4

RUN BEFORE YOU SWIM

"I came here to be a diver," said a trainee in the Navy's Basic Underwater Demolition School (BUDS)."All I've done since I got here is run."

It was true. No part of the United States Armed Forces requires as much physical fitness as the U.S. Navy's elite Underwater Demolition Teams (UDT) and the Sea Air Land (SEAL) forces.

And during the first few weeks of training, the men who volunteer for BUDS run. Then they have more physical training (PT), and then they may run some more.

"We never promised them a rose garden," one instructor said, laughing.

Dressed in green fatigues, the men who want to join UDT must first prove their physical fitness. As they're proving that, they begin learning the rest of the jobs they will have. Then they have to put it together and show that they are as tough mentally as they are physically.

"The only reason a man comes to BUDS is that he wants to," said Captain Norman H. Olson, Commander of the Naval Special Warfare Group in the Atlantic Ocean area. "We don't go out and choose our men. The jobs they may have to do take a special kind of a person. And there aren't many of these people around."

"I worked hard to get myself into shape before I went to BUDS," said one volunteer. "I ran a lot. I got into PT of all different kinds. When they finally sent me to Coronado I thought I could make it with no sweat.

"Boy, was I wrong!"

"We start by not asking the men to do anything we can't, and don't, do ourselves," said an instructor at the demolition school in Coronado, California. "Every instructor here has gone through BUDS and made the team.

"Part of our job is to stay fit, and we do. We have to, if we want to stay on the team. If the trainees have to run five miles, I run right along with them. If they're out swimming, I'm with them.

"This isn't an outfit where we say, 'Do as I say.' It's an outfit where we say, 'Do as I do.' "

It takes 26 weeks of training to make a member of a UDT team. But not all those who go into training come out on the team.

"There have been times when more than half of the men who started training didn't finish it," one team member said. "In the group I trained with, two men out of every five didn't finish. They reached a point where they couldn't go on."

"And there are some who say after a while, 'This is not for me' and drop out," an instructor added. "Every man knows that it's no disgrace not to finish. I admire every person who wants to come to BUDS no matter whether he gets through all 26 weeks.

"For every man who gets into the school there are hundreds who don't even try. So anyone who just *wants to come here is special.*"

"If I'm so special, why are they making me work so hard?" asked a trainee.

"Look at it this way," the instructor said. "We're in the Navy together and I won't always be your instructor. Maybe I'll be your team leader one day. Then I may have to depend on you.

"I want to be sure I *can* depend on you," he added. "We have no way of knowing how that might happen, but you are trying to join a team. Teams play football and basketball. Our job may be different but we're still a team. That means that whatever we do, we do it together. Understand?"

"I understand," the trainee smiled.

"You," said the instructor, "are a week or two into BUDS. You're finding out how hard it can be. It's not as hard yet as it's going to be. But when it's over, you'll see that there is a reason for everything we do. Now do you understand that?"

"I think so," said the trainee.

"It's this simple," the instructor said. "Say we're out on a run. I'm with you, and all of a sudden I yell, 'DUCK!' What do you do?"

"Duck, I guess," said the trainee.

"Suppose we were in some kind of action. Maybe someone had been shooting at us. What happens if I yell then?"

"I duck."

"Right," smiled the instructor, "because you know what would happen if you didn't, right?"

"I might be hurt," said the trainee.

"Wouldn't you rather have a mouthful of sand than an injury of some kind?" the instructor asked.

"Any time," laughed the trainee.

"That's part of the training," said the instructor. "To help you save your own neck and maybe the necks of your teammates. If you hear someone yell 'duck' or any number of things, and you stop to ask why, you might get hurt.

"And you can't be as much help to us if and when you get hurt."

Any man in the Navy can volunteer for the UDT and SEAL teams. He first has to pass through the BUDS training. If there are openings later on he can go into training again and, if he passes, join the SEALs, who also are known as the special warfare group.

"Most UDT men these days get the SEAL training, no matter whether they wind up in a SEAL unit," one officer said.

"Our UDT men are, you could say, trained for action on land and on, in, and under the water. The SEAL teams are parachutists as well, and darned good ones."

And once a man joins the SEAL force he can join one more team—the 'Chuting Stars, otherwise known as the Navy Parachute Team.

"HALF FISH, HALF NUTS"

Until the 1940s, men could not swim underwater for long periods of time. It was not because they didn't want to dive and stay down; they did. They couldn't.

Captain Jacques Yves Cousteau of France changed all that. He invented a valve which could be put on a small tank of air. This valve made it possible for a man using the air tank to breathe air at the same pressure, no matter how deep his dive.

Men had tried to dive before, carrying their own supplies of air. It was dangerous and many of them died. Many more were crippled.

During World War II, some Italians became the first underwater demolitions men. They were called "limpeteers." They were named after a small seashell which looks like a spoutless funnel. The limpet fastens itself to a surface and hangs on.

But the "limpets" the Italians carried were rigged with explosives. They would ride a torpedo-like carrier until they were under a ship. There they would attach their explosive limpets. Then they had to hope their carrier would get them a safe distance away before the explosives went off.

UDT swimmers practice an underwater exit from a submarine.

The first Navy UDT men were called "frogmen," and the name still sticks today. They were sent in before other United States forces landed on a beach. They had to find out if the enemy—or Mother Nature—had put anything in the way. If there were hazards, they blew them up.

After a landing site was cleared, the Navy would send landing craft and landing ships in with their cargoes of men, supplies, and vehicles. By then, most of the frogmen were back on their ships. Their jobs were done.

The UDT men began their missions before Captain Cousteau had perfected his invention. Some could not hide under the water. Some even paddled small rubber rafts to the beaches, then jumped out and waded around to see if there were hazards. Many did not make it back from their missions.

Still, men volunteered for UDT. A school was established at Camp Perry in Virginia to train them. More than half of the men who volunteered for UDT in World War II were killed in action.

"The UDT school has always been tough," said Captain Olson. "Some of our first training groups passed only forty men out of every one hundred who volunteered.

"But that was wartime. Since Would War II, we have had periods of peace. In those times, we like to think of ourselves as keepers of the peace and not as warriors. Still, the two go hand-in-hand."

One of the early problems the UDT men faced came when they began to use Captain Cousteau's valve.

"We knew from the hard-hat divers that you could only go so deep and stay so long before you had problems," a UDT man said. "When you dive, your body is compressed by the weight of the water over you. We knew that sponge divers often got 'the bends' when they came up from the bottom.

"The bends are caused by gases making tiny bubbles in the bloodstream; they can kill or cripple a person. Much of our early diving was experimental. We didn't know what our limits were and we had to find them."

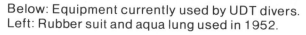
Below: Equipment currently used by UDT divers.
Left: Rubber suit and aqua lung used in 1952.

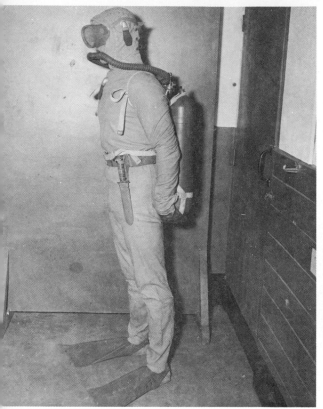

WIDE WORLD PHOTOS

A piece of clothing called a "dry suit" was developed later. UDT men tested it. The dry suit was supposed to keep a man comfortable while he swam in cold water. The first ones didn't work. They were hard to put on and they slowed down a swimmer.

In time, UDT men and SCUBA divers everywhere began to wear a new piece of clothing, the "wet suit." Now, men can dive in water that is too cold for safety and survive.

"We kind of played it by ear," said a man who belonged to UDT in the early fifties. "We'd have an idea, then we'd go out and try it. If it worked, it became part of our training. If it didn't, we'd look for something else.

"There was a tremendous feeling of brotherhood in the early days of UDT. We knew we were working in a new area—just like the scouts on the Western Frontier. We were eager to find new gear and new ways of doing things. When we found them, and they worked, that made it all the better."

Then, in the late 1950s, another idea began to hatch. The Army used its Airborne troops to stage surprise attacks during wars. Why couldn't the Navy, using a small, well-trained force, drop swimmers from aircraft to stage their own surprises? UDT was joined by the SEAL forces.

In the 1960s, Captain Olson decided that the SEALs should have its own parachute demonstration team. The 'Chuting Stars were born.

"Some of our early 'Chuting Stars were veterans of the Korean action," Captain Olson said. "Most of them were young men at the time of Korea who stayed in the Navy and made a career of it.

"Then in the sixties, we fought in Vietnam. Many, if not most, of our SEAL team members—and therefore 'Chuting Stars—saw service in Vietnam."

"The guys who were in Vietnam and who jump at shows should be glad they don't have to wear their glory bars (decorations for valor) when they jump," laughed a former SEAL.

"If they had to wear them, every one would carry too much additional weight. The aircraft might not get off the ground."

"OF MY OWN FREE WILL"

The SEAL team member wore three rows of decorations and a special gold badge over the pocket of his blue uniform coat. Sitting across the desk from him was a sailor.

"You saw the movie and you have heard what I had to say about your training?" the SEAL said.

"Yes, sir," said the sailor.

"You don't have to call me 'sir,' " said the SEAL. "See? I'm a third-class petty officer like you are. But you know that what you are getting into is going to be hard, don't you?"

"I do," said the sailor.

"You are a hospital corpsman, aren't you?" The sailor nodded. "That's good," said the SEAL. "We need more corpsmen ... more medics ... but you realize, don't you, that you won't get any special deals from BUDS or the UDT if you finish?"

"I don't want any," said the sailor. "And if you'll look at my record you'll see I was a medic with the Marine Corps in 'Nam."

15

"You've been through that too?" said the SEAL.

"I sure have," said the sailor, and the two men smiled.

"Some people have said that BUDS is hell on earth," said the SEAL. "Even if you're the tiniest bit afraid of what might happen or what you might do, I warn you against signing this paper and volunteering."

"I know what I'm doing," said the sailor. "I don't know if I can make it all the way through, but I want to try."

"Why?"

"Two reasons," said the sailor. "The biggest reason is that I always wanted to join this group. I have a couple of friends in UDT. I like drawing the extra pay, and I think this is an outfit with a lot of prestige.

"The other reason is my own. I'd like to think I'm as tough as any man. If I can prove that I'm as tough as you, I'll be right, won't I?"

"That's for sure," the SEAL smiled. "You know, don't you, that going to BUDS at Coronado is like being back in boot camp, only worse?"

Left: A heavy, rubber loop is used to haul divers back into the raft.
Below: Divers roll off the raft into the water.

"I know," said the sailor.

"Are you a good swimmer?"

"Pretty good, I think," said the sailor. "I like to swim. I swim whenever I can. I run, too, at least three miles a day and sometimes more. Can I sign the paper now?"

"Not yet," said the SEAL. "What I'm doing is trying to give you the worst possible picture of who we are and what we do. I'm trying to scare you. If, when I'm done, I haven't scared you, I'll let you sign. Fair enough?"

"Look," said the sailor. "My mind is made up. It has been made up for several months, when I first put in for BUDS. It hasn't changed at all."

Helicopters are used to deliver and pick up divers.

"Have a family, Joe?" the SEAL asked.

"You have all the dope on me in front of you, don't you?" said the sailor. "No, I don't have a family. Why do you ask?"

"What do you think?" asked the SEAL. "We aren't exactly against family men, but we'd like to know if you have that in mind. That can make a difference in your thinking, you know."

"I suppose it can. Are there family men in the UDT and SEALs?"

"A few. Most of them have gotten married long after they joined, however. Please don't get me wrong. Having a family doesn't make you wrong for the teams any more than not having a family makes you right for them. When did you have your last physical?"

"Six or eight months ago," the sailor said.

"You're healthy? Did you get hurt in 'Nam?"

"I'm fine," said the sailor. "I got hit twice in 'Nam, but they were both flesh wounds. I was off the line a total of three weeks for both injuries and that was it."

"You must heal fast," said the SEAL, smiling. "Well, Joe, I can't see any reason for turning you down, but I'm not the person who makes the decisions. All I'm here for today is to make sure you know what you're getting into. Now that I'm sure, I guess you can sign this paper." As he spoke, he shoved the paper and a pen toward the sailor, who signed and pushed it back to the SEAL. The SEAL stuck his hand out; the sailor shook it.

"I hope to see you again soon," said the SEAL. "Good luck and I hope you make it. Remember that it's nothing to be ashamed of if you don't, though."

"I'll make it," grinned the sailor.

TRAINING

Perspiration rolled down the trainees' faces. It darkened the backs of their green jackets.

While an instructor watched, and counted for them, the trainees were working out with large logs. There were six men to a log, and each log was as big around as a telephone pole and about twenty feet long.

On command, the men bent over, putting their hands as far under the logs as they could. Another command, and each group lifted its log until it rested on their knees. Then they straightened up and held the logs at their waists.

For the next half hour, the logs stayed in the hands of the trainees. The logs were lifted overhead, then brought down to shoulder level. They were shifted from shoulder to shoulder.

Each man had to do his part. If he didn't, the team couldn't do what it was told. Eyes bulged, cords stood out on their necks, and even more perspiration appeared, some of it running into the mens' eyes and making them sting.

Then, finally, a command was given. Each of the logs was returned to the ground. The men, weary when they began the log drill, were even more tired. Still, they lined up at the instructor's command and double-timed away from the drill site.

While one group of men worked on the logs, another group was out on the water in rubber rafts. Each wore a heavy steel helmet and a lifejacket. Each had a paddle.

They were trying to paddle their rubber rafts in a straight line toward the beach at Coronado. Some were doing better than others.

"Some groups learn about teamwork faster than others," said their instructor. "If you put six men in a raft and only five paddle, those five have to work harder to make the raft go in a straight line.

"Now I didn't tell them they had to, but all those people out there are racing against each other. You'll hear about it when they hit the beach. The guys who come in last will hear about it from the others."

The first raft hit the beach and its paddlers jumped out. Working as a group they hoisted the raft to their shoulders and trotted up the beach. Even though no one spoke, the men were in step with one another.

When all the rafts were back in storage, the men fell into formation as the instructor came near. Just before, however, he heard those who were first on the beach giving the last men a hard time.

The instructor spoke to the men briefly and dismissed them. Their work was over for the day. All but one of them moved toward their barracks. That one man headed for another building where a bright, brass bell hung in the entrance. He stopped in front of the bell and rang it three times. Then he dropped his belt to the ground and trudged off. The instructor shrugged.

"I kind of expected that," he said. "That man just took himself out of BUDS. They come here of their own free will and they can leave just as freely." The next day, the Navy would begin the work of sending the man to another Navy duty station.

Back on the beach, another group of men was waiting. They watched as, one by one, others—also in green uniforms dark with perspiration—came running back down the beach toward them. As each runner finished, the group roared.

"Timed five-mile run," said the instructor. "It isn't enough that a man can run five miles, he has to be able to run it within a certain period. I'd guess that this group hasn't reached its time limit yet.

"This isn't one chance and one chance only. If any men from this group don't make their time today they'll get another chance. But if they never make the right time, they don't make the team.

"Few fail in this test," he smiled. "If a man's determined enough to get this far in BUDS, he'll probably go all the way."

Elsewhere on the Coronado base, a boat was returning from San Clemente Island, bringing other trainees.

"Those, mostly, are men who have passed the physical part of our training," the instructor said. "They go up to San Clemente for training in one of the more important parts of our job—demolition.

"By the time we're done with that phase of the training, they'll know how to clear beaches, throw hand grenades, and anything else that involves explosives."

Although much of the UDT training occurs on the beach, out of doors, in the water, or on San Clemente, BUDS pupils also go to classrooms.

"There aren't many of us, so every man has to be able to do more than one job," a trainee said. "The man who really knows his explosives has to know first aid almost as well. We do have specialists, but they aren't always available."

DIVING

Swimming becomes part of BUDS training later in the program. By then, the trainees are in top shape and ready for almost anything.

Every person in the Navy must swim before he completes basic training. Navy swimming lessons teach not just how to swim, but how to use life jackets in the water, how to jump into the water from high places, and how to use one's clothing to help in floating if life jackets aren't available.

"Swimming is a very important part of our job," said a BUDS instructor. "Our men have to be able to go into the water, swim a long distance, do a job, and swim back."

Swims of two miles are common in BUDS.

"I thought a five-mile run was tough at first," said a trainee. "When we had to make that run against the clock it didn't seem too bad. But I think I'd rather run five miles than swim two miles. Swimming can take a lot out of you."

"By the time a man finishes BUDS he's probably swum more miles than most people do in a lifetime," said an instructor. "He'll keep doing it once he's on the team, too."

Not all swimming is done with the help of the fins that helped UDT men gain the name of "frogmen," either. At first, a trainee must prove he can swim as well, and as efficiently, without them.

Only after the instructors know a trainee is a good swimmer does he go on to diving. Even then, the training with underwater breathing equipment doesn't begin right away.

Students are fitted with masks and given snorkel tubes—U-shaped tubes with a mouthpiece in one end.

"We start by showing them how to swim on the surface using the snorkels," said an instructor. "Some have trouble at first. They find it hard to breathe with their noses and mouths under water."

After a trainee can snorkel well in a swimming pool, he begins making shallow dives in the pool, then coming to the surface again. During the dive the snorkel tube fills with water, but he clears it by blowing air out the tube so he can breathe again.

Only when a man is comfortable with the snorkel does he go on to SCUBA (Self-Contained Underwater Breathing Apparatus). And even though the Pacific Ocean is only a short distance away, the first SCUBA work is done in a swimming pool.

"There's much more to SCUBA diving than just putting on the gear and jumping in," a trainee said. "For one thing if you dive into the water head-first with the gear on, the water's likely to rip some of it off. So you learn to flop in on your back, or to jump flat-footed with your fins on and let them slow you down."

In the pool, everyone learns to use three different underwater breathing systems.

"Almost as important is their learning what the limits are in diving. Everyone knows you can stay down only as long as your air lasts," said an instructor. "You can make your air last longer if you don't work too hard. The smoother you work underwater, the less oxygen you'll use.

"The men learn what to do if one of their buddies runs out of air and can't go to the surface. In that case, he'll share the air supply of another man. It isn't easy for a man to take his mouthpiece out and hand it to another guy in 50 feet of water, but everyone gets used to the idea."

When SCUBA diving began in the late 1940s and early 1950s, people knew it was dangerous to dive too deeply, but no one knew just how dangerous or just how deep.

"The U.S. Navy didn't write the book on deep diving, but it sure did help," one UDT man said. "When all this started we had the desire and the manpower to do this kind of work. Now, what we took a long time to learn in the fifties is down in black and white. We can learn it out of a book with much less risk than the early divers had to take."

The trainees work with the equipment in a pool until their instructors are satisfied that they are ready to dive in open water. When that time comes, the men go back to their rubber rafts and into the Pacific Ocean.

"The big difference is that the Pacific is deeper, colder, and less clean," said a trainee.

Operating in small groups with instructors diving with them and more safety people in boats above them, the trainees make many dives in the Pacific. In time, they become experienced open-water divers and are ready to combine their dive training with the other work they have done in BUDS.

DELIVERY AND PICKUP

Everyone knows how to get into the water, but how does a frogman get out?

"Very quickly, most of the time," a UDT member said, laughing.

"Let's say we have to look over a beach. Our operation might begin just before dawn. We'll get into a boat of some kind and head for that beach, using darkness as our cover.

"It would be nice if the boat could stop and drop each man off, but it doesn't work that way. It would take forever to deliver an entire team, and we seldom have that much time.

"So we put a rubber raft alongside the boat. As the boat moves through the drop area, each man in turn gets into the raft, sits on the edge, and when he's told, he falls over backwards into the water."

The delivery also can be done by helicopter.

"UDTs have begun to use helicopters like some people use taxicabs," said a UDT man. "They are quicker than boats but they're also noisier. Because of the noise they sometimes just don't work."

The helicopter with a team on board will fly slowly over the drop area with its door or tail ramp open. On command, each man jumps, feet-first, into the water from a height of six to ten feet. These techniques also are practiced at BUDS.

Trainees learn to be picked up at high speeds by both boat and helicopter.

"Every mission that goes out should come back," an instructor said. "This means that the UDT men must keep track of time. At the designated time, they should be at the pickup point assigned to them."

A boat, probably the same one that dropped them off, roars into the pickup area. A single man kneels in the rubber raft alongside the boat. He holds a loop made of heavy rubber.

The waiting divers each raise an arm above their heads. Their elbows are bent.

As the boat comes alongside each diver, it doesn't slow down at all. The man in the rubber raft slips his loop over the forearm of the diver as he passes. Then he hauls with all his might.

With one motion, the diver pops out of the water and slides, head-first, into the raft. Once aboard he scrambles out of the raft and onto the boat while the pick-up man readies his loop for the next diver.

"Entire teams can be picked up in a matter of seconds," an instructor said. "This can come in handy if there happens to be a force on the beach who doesn't like us very much."

"The first time I was picked up this way I thought my arm would fall off at the shoulder," a trainee said. "But now that I've done it at least two dozen times, I do believe the arm is there to stay."

"I'd almost rather be picked up by boat," said another trainee. "In that pickup someone else has to do most of the work. With a helicopter, you have to do it all."

When a helicopter is used to pick up a team, it trails a rope ladder some fifteen feet long.

"Even though a chopper can hover, that is often difficult for the pilot. Most of the time, they fly slowly forward during a pickup operation, maybe five to ten knots," an instructor said.

The diver must first get hold of the ladder, or part of it.

"That's when the fun begins," said a trainee. "Five knots isn't fast on land but when you have water dragging at you it's different. The first couple of steps up that ladder are the hardest. It's even worse when you are in full gear with the tank and other stuff. But once you get your feet clear of the water, the hard part is over."

"It's a hard way to end a mission," another trainee said. "Here you've been dropped off, you swim a couple of miles to a target, do your job, and swim those two miles back.

"'You're pooped by then, you know? Then you have to haul yourself ten or fifteen feet into the sky for the flight home. Why couldn't they build choppers with elevators, or maybe even escalators?"

THAT WEEK

One of the last weeks in BUDS is called "Motivation Week." But most of the men who make it that far in training have other words to describe it.

For one group the week began at exactly 2:08 A.M. Monday, when they were rousted out of bed. In ten minutes, they stood in full battle gear in front of their barracks. Their faces were blackened so they would not reflect light.

After a quick march to the docks, they boarded a boat. While they traveled to a nearby beach, they learned what they had to do—stage a mock attack on an "enemy" stronghold.

"These can be called games, but by this time they're serious," an instructor said. "The trainees use real explosives and sometimes even live ammunition in these exercises. People can get hurt if someone makes a mistake. By this time, however, there are very few mistakes."

It was still dark when the men finished their job. Tired, they returned to their barracks just in time for reveille—the beginning of the military day. There was just barely time to change uniforms and fall in for chow.

"In this week we push everyone to the limit. We have to. We are not trying to break them, nor are we trying to force them out at this point. This is their last test. Once a man has gone through motivation week we know he's ready for anything," said an instructor.

"We don't just get in shape and learn different things," said a trainee. "Being able to get through motivation week is a real boost to our self-confidence. We sort of need that, too."

During the week, the trainees were allowed to sleep, but never seemed to catch up on the sleep they lost. They were sent out to run—or swim—for an hour or more even before they got to sleep. They ran obstacle courses, fired weapons, and lifted logs. They paddled their assault rafts and ran some more.

"They just don't leave you alone very long," said a trainee. "You start to count the days left in this week but then you get so worn down you lose count."

"I don't think I ever stayed dry for more than an hour or two at a time during my motivation week," a UDT member said. "The experience was kind of a hell on earth—a lot of us still call it 'hell week'—but I sure learned I could go and go and go in spite of myself."

Near the end of the week, the trainees spend almost a full day in a mudhole.

Trainee turns a somersault in mud during motivation week. Only about two-thirds of the trainees make it to this phase of the training program.

WIDE WORLD PHCTOS

"Not a foxhole, mind you, but a big hole in the ground waist deep in mud which is a little thicker than tomato soup," a trainee explained.

"The mud gets into your clothing, into your eyes, nose, and mouth, and into your boots. After a while you get so cold that all you want to do is sit and shiver. No kid who ever made mud pies ever got so dirty.

"Then they make you do things in the mud. You're working all the time. When you try to stand up you slip and fall in deeper. After I was done in the hole I spent a week tasting mud before things started to taste normal again."

"Two hours in the hole and I was ready to climb out and quit," said another UDT member. "But then I said to myself, 'Look. You've gone this far. Are you going to quit over a little mud?' I stuck it out. Stick it out is a good way to describe the hole, too."

After the mudhole the trainees were marched back to their barracks. The first clean-up was done with a hose. After that, they showered the dirt off their bodies, grateful for the warm water of the showers.

"I knew this was coming," said a trainee. "I was afraid of it, in a way, and I didn't like it while I was doing it. But I've done it now and it's over. I made it. I'm almost warm again.

"I feel great!"

ON TO BENNING!

Graduation from BUDS is, for most UDT men, the proudest moment of their lives.

They now can join one of the Navy's UDT teams somewhere in the United States or elsewhere in the world. Some will go back to the special tasks they had before they became UDT men. All will wear the special UDT badge.

"You can tell that most other Navy men look at someone who wears the badge with a different attitude," said a UDT member. "They have more respect for us because almost everyone knows what we had to go through to earn the badge."

NAVAL SPECIAL WARFARE

There are other schools UDT men can go to and many choose "jump school." The Navy doesn't have enough parachutists to justify having its own jump school, so UDT men join the Army for training at Fort Benning, Georgia, the Army jump school.

"We take a fair amount of kidding from the Army when we go," said a UDT member. "But none of them get serious about it because they know what our training has been like. At least some of the men we train with are Army Rangers and other special forces men; they've had some of the same stuff."

"The Army's routine is to start their men on PT and get on to the jump training later," a SEAL laughed.

"That training, for most UDT men, is not much harder than getting out of bed in the morning. At least, it wasn't for me."

In four weeks' time, the men get their basic parachute training, including jumping from airplanes with groups. These are called "static line" jumps because their 'chutes are opened by a cord tied both to the rip cord of the parachute and the aircraft.

"It depends on the training that's available at the time, but most of our men go on to make many free-fall jumps," another SEAL said. "In these jumps the man pulls his own rip cord after falling anywhere from two to five thousand feet.

"Each jump is watched closely by instructors. If a man does something wrong which could hurt him in another situation, he hears about it right away. Once our jump training is completed, we can go from UDT to the Sea Air Land (SEAL) Team."

SEALs, then, are frogmen who fly. They may jump from a helicopter six to ten feet above water; they may jump from an aircraft at ten thousand feet. Some even go to school to learn how to jump from an aircraft flying so high it can't be heard on the ground.

"These high-altitude jumps require an oxygen supply because the air is too thin where we bail out," said a SEAL. "We breathe from the oxygen bottle until we are ten to fifteen thousand feet over ground, and that's where the atmosphere is thick enough to breathe again."

"It's a kick," said a SEAL. "High-altitude jumping is very cold—sometimes the air when you jump will be way below zero. But you float through the sky for an incredible length of time before you have to open your 'chute. It's almost like diving in water, even if you're falling very fast.

"As you get lower the air warms up. By the time your
'chute opens it's maybe only ten to fifteen degrees cooler than
it is on the ground. Meanwhile you've made a trip of three
or four miles—maybe more—almost straight down."

All SEALs have one more privilege. They are eligible to
become 'Chuting Stars, or members of the Navy's elite
Parachute Team.

THE 'CHUTING STARS

"I jump in shows because I like to meet people," said a member of the Navy Parachute Team. "I really don't need the recognition."

Each year, operating both from Coronado and from Little Creek, Virginia, 'Chuting Star teams fan out across the country. They demonstrate the Navy's ability at parachuting, just as the Golden Knights do for the Army.

"We aren't out to show them up or anything," said a team member. "Our demonstration is a little different from theirs, of course, but we could do what they do if we wanted to, and they could copy us, too."

The demonstration team usually includes ten men, one of whom is the team leader. Each man may have to take up to two hundred pounds of equipment when he travels to a show, including a parachute, a reserve parachute, jump helmet, boots, gloves, personal clothing, and other gear.

"Like a lot of other military teams we will, at times, spend long times on the road," said a SEAL. "We don't always fly out, do a show and come right back to our base. Long trips can be tiresome, but we usually have more than enough men to go when we're set for a show."

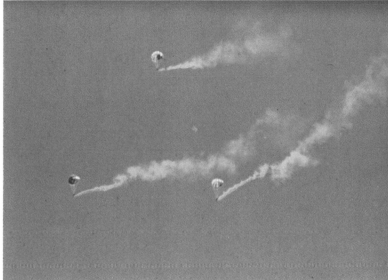

Flag jumps often begin many air shows, " and we do them like everyone else," said a SEAL. "Others in the team often go up at the same time as the flag jumper because our part of an air show comes early lots of times."

No specific aircraft has been assigned to the 'Chuting Stars, but if they are jumping at a Navy airfield that's no problem.

"Sometimes, when we are at a civilian show, the sponsor provides the plane," a member said. "We have jumped from all different kinds of aircraft over the years. You have to change the way you leave the plane in some cases, but that's no problem."

'Chuting Star members trade jobs in the demonstrations. The man who does the "cutaway" jump—opening, then streamering and cutting away a parachute that's not working—may be the flag jumper in the next.

"The cutaway jump draws a lot of ohs and ahs. Most people applaud when the second 'chute opens," a member said. "But my favorite for the oh and ah department is the demonstration we do of free fall technique.

"In this one, one of us takes the usual belly down, arms out free fall position after he leaves the aircraft. The other man just dives headfirst, and because there's less air resistance, he falls much faster.

"So one of the guys is kind of floating down to the point where he opens his 'chute and the other is coming like a ton of bricks. It's a good demonstration."

Other 'Chuting Star demonstration jumps include a show of how a free-falling jumper can "fly" in different directions, formation jumps, and even stars, in which many jumpers try to link up during free fall to give the appearance of a star.

'Chuting Stars most often jump for Navy shows, but they can be seen at shows performed by civilian and other military groups.

"We get some sailors interested in UDT and SEAL when we jump at Navy shows," said a SEAL. "And I hope we get some people not in the Navy interested in joining the Navy as well.

"Most of us didn't join the Navy because the United States was drafting people for the Armed Forces. We joined because we wanted to join.

"The Navy has been good to me. In one more year I'll have enough work done for a college degree. And in eight more years I can retire, if I want to.

"Maybe they still say, 'Join the Navy and see the world.' That's one of the things that brought me in, and I have seen a lot of the world now. Maybe some of it wasn't the best, but that's the way it works.

"I'm proud to be in the Navy. I'm proud to be a SEAL and I'm proud that I have the chance, by jumping, to show it."

ABOUT THE AUTHOR

Peter B. Mohn has been following the Performers in Uniform since 1971, but it took five years before he thought about writing about them. When not writing books about flight and flying, he fishes the salt waters around Fort Myers, Florida. He's lived there ever since being cured of Minnesota by the winter of 1977.

INDEX

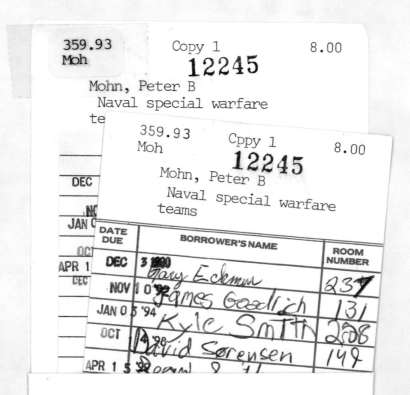

359.93
Moh

Copy 1   8.00

12245

Mohn, Peter B
 Naval special warfare
te

359.93   Cppy 1   8.00
Moh
                         12245
     Mohn, Peter B
      Naval special warfare
teams

DATE DUE	BORROWER'S NAME	ROOM NUMBER
DEC 3 1990	Gary Eckman	237
NOV 1 0 '92	James Goodrich	131
JAN 0 3 '94	Kyle Smith	208
OCT 14 '98	David Sorensen	149
APR 1 5	Sean R.	